W9-CCU-218

SCIENCE
SOLVES IT!

SPORTS CHAMPIONS

LINDA AKSOMITIS

Crabtree Publishing Company
www.crabtreebooks.com

Crabtree Publishing Company
www.crabtreebooks.com

Author: Linda Aksomitis
Project editor: Tom Jackson
Designer: Lynne Lennon
Picture researcher: Sophie Mortimer
Indexer: Kay Ollerenshaw
Managing editor: Miranda Smith
Art director: Jeni Child
Design manager: David Poole
Editorial director: Lindsey Lowe
Children's publisher: Anne O'Daly
Editor: Michael Hodge
Proofreaders: Adrianna Morganelli, Crystal Sikkens
Project coordinator: Robert Walker
Production coordinator: Katherine Kantor
Font management: Mike Golka
Prepress technician: Katherine Kantor

This edition published in 2009 by
Crabtree Publishing Company.

The Brown Reference Group plc,
First Floor, 9–17 St. Albans Place,
London, N1 0NX
www.brownreference.com

Copyright © 2009 The Brown Reference Group plc

Photographs:
Action Plus: Leo Mason: p. 25 (top), 28–29
Alamy: Ashley Cooper: p. 22 (bottom)
BRG: p. 9 (left and right)
Corbis: Duomo: p. 7 (bottom), 8, 10 (left); Karl-Josef
    Hildenbrand: p. 11; Dimitri Iundt: p. 6 (bottom); Olivier
    Labalette: p. 24 (bottom); Reuters: p. 26 (right); Jean-Yves
    Rusznlewski: p. 19 (top), 20 (bottom); TWPhoto: p. 16–17
Getty Images: Robert E. Daemmrich: p. 15 (bottom); Julian
    Finney: p. 28 (bottom); Richard Heathcote: p. 29 (bottom)
PA Photos: Tony Marshall: p. 14 (bottom); Denis Poroy: p. 21;
    Martial Trezzini: p. 25 (bottom), 27 (top)
Rex Features: Giuliano Bevilacqua: p. 27 (bottom)
Science Photo Library: Phillipe Plailly: cover
Shutterstock: Andresr: p. 12–13; Galina Barskaya: p. 6–7;
    Loris Eichenberger: p. 12 (bottom); Elena Elisseeva:
    p. 13 (bottom); Jackie Foster: p. 13 (top), 16 (left); Jeff
    Hinds: p. 5; Matthew Jacques: p. 24–25; Jonathan Larsen:
    p. 18 (bottom), 22–23; Tomas Loutocky: p. 17 (top); Byron
    W. Moore: p. 4–5; Sean Nel: p. 20 (top); Michael Pettigrew:
    p. 26 (bottom); Solid Web Designs Ltd.: p. 7 (top), 10 (right);
    Tootles: p. 18–19; visi.stock: p. 23 (bottom); Dmitry Yashkin:
    p. 14–15

Every effort has been made to trace the owners of
copyrighted material.

Library and Archives Canada Cataloguing in Publication

Aksomitis, Linda
       Sports champions / Linda Aksomitis.

(Science solves it)
Includes index.
ISBN 978-0-7787-4172-5 (bound).–ISBN 978-0-7787-4179-4 (pbk.)

       1. Sports sciences–Juvenile literature. 2. Sports–Technological
innovations–Juvenile literature. I. Title. II. Series: Science solves
it (St. Catharines, Ont.)

GV558.A58 2008   j613.7'1   C2008-905000-2

Library of Congress Cataloging-in-Publication Data

Aksomitis, Linda.
   Sports champions / Linda Aksomitis.
       p. cm. – (Science solves it)
   Includes index.
   ISBN-13: 978-0-7787-4179-4 (pbk. : alk. paper)
   ISBN-10: 0-7787-4179-6 (pbk. : alk. paper)
   ISBN-13: 978-0-7787-4172-5 (reinforced library binding : alk. paper)
   ISBN-10: 0-7787-4172-9 (reinforced library binding : alk. paper)
   1. Sports sciences–Juvenile literature. 2. Sports–Technological innovations–
Juvenile literature. I. Title. II. Series.

   GV558.A57 2009
   613.7'1–dc22
                                                                    2008034150

Crabtree Publishing Company
www.crabtreebooks.com   1-800-387-7650

**Published in Canada
Crabtree Publishing**
616 Welland Ave.
St. Catharines, ON
L2M 5V6

**Published in the United States
Crabtree Publishing**
PMB16A
350 Fifth Ave., Suite 3308
New York, NY 10118

CONTENTS

WHAT IS SPORTS SCIENCE?

Sports science helps the world's athletes become champions. Sports science can help you be a winner, too.

Coaches use sports science to plan practices. Sports science helps your family choose healthy foods. It also helps companies make better sports equipment. There are many different areas of sports science. Biology explains how your body works. Chemistry gives you an understanding of how food gives you energy. Physics helps you understand how you stay upright on a skateboard or how to curve a soccer ball into the net! **Psychologists** also teach top sports stars how to set goals and feel like winners. That helps them focus on training for big competitions.

Runners are helped by science in many ways. It is used to design running shoes and make refreshing sports drinks.

IMPRESSIVE ATHLETICISM

One of the world's hardest athletic competitions is the decathlon at the Olympic Games. The decathlon is a two-day event. Athletes run races of 100, 400, and 1,500 meters. They also compete in the 110-meter hurdles, the long jump, the high jump, the shot put, the discus, the javelin, and the pole vault (pictured). To win, a decathlete must be very good at all ten events. And sports science is there to help athletes do their best.

BODYWORKS

The human body is a living machine.
It must be kept healthy to run well.
Sports science helps to understand how
to keep your body strong and powerful.

Whatever sport you play, the key body systems involved are the same—the muscles, the heart, and the lungs. But don't forget the brain. This is the body's control center. It uses the information from your senses to make quick decisions. Sometimes you have to think about what to do— whether to pass the ball or speed up at the end of a race. These are **conscious** decisions. The brain also makes **unconscious** decisions. For example, you start sweating or breathe quicker during a hard workout, decisions that your brain makes for you.

MUSCLE TYPES

The muscles used during sports are called **voluntary** muscles. You control these muscles. Sometimes these muscles work on their own. Most of your other muscles are involuntary. These work the stomach, intestines, or lungs. They are working even when you are asleep.

HEART PUMP

The muscles of your heart never rest. They pump blood through your body every minute of every day. As the heart pumps , you can feel its beats through the **pulse** in your wrist. It is important to keep your heart muscles healthy and strong.

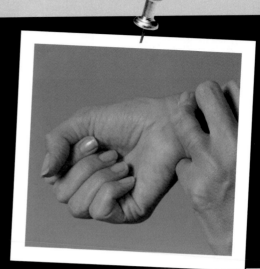

The human body is your most important piece of sports equipment.

FUEL SUPPLY

The heart and lungs are the fuel pumps of the body. They provide muscles with **oxygen** and food.

MUSCLE POWER

Our bones may keep us straight, but without muscles, we wouldn't be able to move. There are about 600 different muscles in the human body. They are attached to joints by tough strings called **tendons**.

Muscles work by contracting, or becoming shorter. As the muscle contracts, it pulls on a bone, making it move.

REAL LIFE

There are two types of **muscle fiber**—slow-twitch and fast-twitch. Basketball players use slow-twitch muscles to keep running up and down the court at a steady speed. When they need a short burst of strength to jump up to dunk the ball, the players use their fast-twitch muscles. Athletes train in certain ways to build up their different types of muscle fibers.

Exercise tears the muscle fibers very slightly. You feel stiff after this happens. As they repair themselves, the muscles grow back slightly larger. Over time, you develop bigger, stronger muscles.

A muscle is made of many bundles of **fibers**. These fibers shrink in length to make the muscle contract after receiving an electric signal from the brain. This signal travels along a **nerve**. The electricity passes down the nerve and into the muscle thanks to salt-like **minerals** inside. If the muscle runs out of these minerals, it stops working properly. That is when you might get a muscle cramp.

The bones of the skeleton are covered by a layer of muscles. The muscles work together to move the bones.

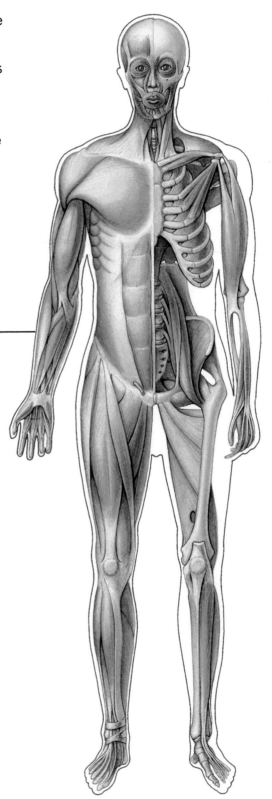

EXAMINE THE FACTS

Muscles work in pairs to move different parts of the body. One muscle pulls one way, and the other pulls in the opposite direction. The best examples are in your arms. The biceps on the front of your upper arm bend your arm at the elbow. The triceps on the back of the upper arm, straighten the arm again. How many other muscle pairs can you find in your body?

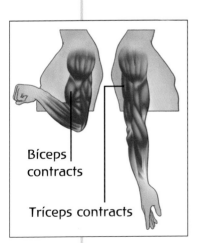

Biceps contracts

Triceps contracts

The body needs oxygen from the air to power the muscles. Air is collected by the lungs. The oxygen that travels into the lungs is then picked up by blood. The blood carries oxygen around the body, pushed along by the heart.

FUELING CELLS

Body **cells** use oxygen to release energy from food. During sports, your muscles work harder so you can keep up with the other competitors. As a result, your muscles need more oxygen. So you breathe faster, and your heart beats more quickly. An athlete trains to make sure his or her heart and lungs will supply enough oxygen when needed.

Take your resting pulse: hold a finger firmly over your wrist and count the number of heartbeats in 10 seconds. Then play soccer or some other fast sport for 15 minutes. Take your pulse again. Is it quicker or slower? When your cells need more energy, they use more oxygen. Blood must be pumped faster through your body to get the oxygen to where it is needed, so your pulse rate goes up.

A weightlifter's muscles burn a lot of fuel very quickly during a lift. They do it without using oxygen. That makes weightlifting an **anaerobic** sport.

OXYGEN LIMIT

> The body produces EPO to build more red blood cells. The more blood cells you have, the more oxygen your body can carry.

VO_2 is short for "volume of oxygen." It is the maximum amount of oxygen a body can hold. Men have a higher VO_2 than women. As athletes train and condition their bodies, their VO_2 gets higher. An average untrained person has a VO_2 max of 45, and with training can get it to 60. Cross-country skiers have a very high VO_2. The Norwegian skier Espen Harald Bjerke has a VO_2 of 96 — the highest ever measured.

When muscles work using oxygen it is called **aerobic** exercise. Jogging is an aerobic sport. However, when muscles need a huge burst of energy, there is no time to get oxygen to them. So they do it without oxygen. This is anaerobic exercise, and it makes muscles get tired very quickly.

The body produces EPO (short for erythropoietin) when it needs to build more blood cells. The more blood cells you have, the more oxygen you can carry. Athletes sometimes inject extra EPO so they can perform better and for longer. This is illegal in sports because it is dangerous and unfair.

FOOD FOR FUEL

Your energy comes from food. Athletes have special diets so they can keep winning week after week.

Some of the food athletes eat helps them build strong and flexible muscles. Other food gives them the power they need to perform in a big game or race. Sports science helps athletes understand how their bodies use different types of food.

Athletes cannot develop strong muscles without training hard. Some athletes take drugs to make their muscles grow stronger faster. It is very dangerous to use these drugs, and it is not fair for other athletes. Drugs are banned in all sports, but many athletes are allowed to take other helpful food **supplements**.

SUGAR RUSH

Carbohydrate is the main source of energy for muscles. Carbohydrates include sugars and starches, such as bread and potatoes. Athletes use carbohydrate drinks and gels during exercise, or right after it, to give them a boost of energy. Athletes also eat meals full of carbohydrates—such as a large plate of pasta—a few hours before a long race or big training day.

THIRSTY WORK

Athletes need to drink water to perform well. The body needs a lot of water to work properly and keep cool when working at full speed. Sports drinks are designed to get water and salts to the muscles and nerves very fast during a competition.

Athletes need to eat a mix of foods to build strong bodies.

BUILDING UP

Muscles are made from **proteins**. An athlete's diet has to be rich in protein so he or she can build stronger muscles. A good source of protein is meat, which is the muscle of another animal. However, there are other sources of protein. Eight ounces (225 g) of yogurt contains about 20 percent of the protein and 30 percent of the **calcium** you need each day. Calcium is used to make strong bones.

BODY MASS

The Body Mass Index (BMI) compares your weight with your height. It is calculated by dividing weight in kilograms by the square of height (height multiplied by itself) in meters. If you are overweight, you have a high BMI. However, muscle weighs more than fat. Big athletes, such as football and rugby players, may have a high BMI. They are still very healthy people.

An off-road cyclist collects a banana during a long race. The banana has carbohydrates for energy and the minerals needed to keep muscles working.

FOOD TYPES

You likely have favorite foods, but are they rich in **nutrients**? Will they help you become a better athlete? Every food contains different nutrients. Meat, fish, eggs, and beans provide protein. Your body needs protein to build healthy muscles.

Carbohydrates provide fuel for your brain and muscles. Sweet-tasting sugars are known as simple carbohydrates. They include glucose and sucrose. Fruits like apples, oranges, and bananas contain a lot of simple carbohydrates. Complex carbohydrates are not sweet. Foods like pasta, rice, and breakfast cereal contain a lot of this food type. Your body must break them up into simpler carbohydrates to release the energy stored inside.

Your body needs fat to be healthy. Good fats are **unsaturated**. They come from foods like avocados, olives, and most nuts. **Saturated** fats are sometimes called bad fats. They are in butter, cheese, and red meat. Too much saturated fat in the body makes it unhealthy.

EXAMINE THE FACTS

Keep a food diary; write down everything you eat for one week. Then compare what you have eaten with the advice on a government food guide, such as *www.mypyramid.gov*. Did you eat foods from all the groups? How can you improve your diet by eating different fruits and new types of foods?

EXTRA SUPPLIES

Your body also needs **vitamins**. These are chemicals that your body cannot make by itself. It needs a supply of about 20 vitamins to work properly. Fruits, nuts, and vegetables are good sources of vitamins and minerals. You need to eat a wide range. Brightly colored fruits and vegetables are usually richest in vitamins and minerals.

TOO HEAVY

Junk food, such as burgers and fries, contains mostly fat and carbohydrates. If your body does not use all of what you eat, it will store it as fat. You gradually get heavier. Forty percent of North American teens are too heavy to be healthy.

DRINK UP

An athlete weighs less after training. That is because his or her body has lost water by sweating. For every lost pound, athletes must drink two or three cups of fluid to rehydrate the body. Water is normally best. However, if an athlete has trained for more than one hour he or she can use sports drinks to replace lost minerals, too.

Sumo wrestlers need to be heavy to win. Most are more than 300 pounds (136 kg) and have a traditional high-protein diet.

EATING RIGHT

You must eat the right foods to provide energy for what you do. A top golfer will not need the same diet as a figure skater. They burn different amounts of energy. Sports nutritionists help athletes decide what foods they should eat.

All athletes need to drink a lot of liquids. They lose water when sweating. If they run low on water, they become **dehydrated**. That affects their concentration and skills. Sports drinks contain minerals and sugars. The minerals keep the muscles and nerves working. The sugar provides a boost of energy.

SPORTS DRINKS

The effect of sports drinks has been shown by sports scientists. One group of cyclists drank a sports drink containing sugars and minerals. Another group drank water that was flavored to taste the same. The cyclists then all went around the same course. The average time for those who had drank the sports drink was 2.3 percent faster than the cyclists who drank water. Their team would have won the race!

CHEAT EATS

Many serious athletes are allowed to take supplements that help with training. However, some substances are banned because they are unfair. The illegal substances are sometimes called **steroids**. They work in the same way as the body's **hormones**. Steroids are dangerous. If athletes take too many, they will damage their bodies, not make them stronger! Steve Bechler, a pitcher for the Baltimore Orioles, died of heat stroke in 2003. Taking steroids was part of the cause.

TRAINING TIME

To be the best, athletes have to train a lot. Training keeps their bodies fit for competitions. Training also lets them learn new skills and get even better at old ones.

It takes years of training to become a top athlete. The first thing to do is learn the basic skills of the sport. You have to learn how to hold a baseball bat before you can swing. The coach pitches easy balls for you to learn how to hit. The teams throw the baseball back and forth to practice catching.

Even major-league stars must practice. Practice strengthens the muscles you will use in games. As your muscles get stronger, you can throw the ball farther, and you can run around the bases faster.

AIMING HIGH

Athletes set goals. Goal setting gives them an idea of what they want to achieve in their careers. That helps them get **motivated** to train hard. It is important for athletes to have realistic goals that they can achieve regularly. Reaching these goals gives them self-esteem and helps them focus on the next competition.

PREPARATION

An athlete has a training program that prepares him or her for a big competition —perhaps the start of the football season or even the Olympic Games. The program is designed to develop the athlete's strength, skills, and desire to win.

MIX IT UP

The best training programs involve lots of different exercises. This is called cross-training. Each exercise works a different set of muscles. Adding new types of exercises increases overall fitness. Cross-training reduces the risk of injuries. It also helps keep athletes from becoming bored with training.

A high school football coach gives a team talk during a training session.

BODY MOVES

Practice is the key to success. The coach's job is to help you develop your fitness and skills. When you get to practice, the coach assigns drills. The drill matches your job in the team or is designed to prepare you for the next competition.

Kinesiology is the branch of science that studies how the body moves in sports. There are many factors that affect how your body can move. Girls are generally more flexible than boys, but boys are normally stronger. The right kinds of practice can increase **flexibility** as well as strength.

Ballet dancers practice in a studio with a large mirror. The mirror allows the dancer to watch herself dance.

Throwing a javelin requires a good **technique** as well as strength. This photograph shows the shapes the body makes during a throw. The coach can use the picture to point out ways of improving technique.

REAL LIFE

Tony Hawk (right) has spent a lifetime practicing. At 16, he was the best skateboarder in the world. Over the next 17 years, he won 73 skateboard competitions. Hawk did the first 900 trick in skateboarding competition history in 1999. The 900 trick is a 900 degree spin, or two and a half rotations in the air.

BRAIN TRAIN

During practice, your body is being trained to move in certain ways. Your brain is also learning. Scientists have investigated how the brain works during practice by studying ballet dancers. They recorded a dancer's brain activity while he watched ballet on a video. When he saw a move he already knew how to do, the dancer's brain responded to it in the same way as if he was actually dancing. However, his brain did not do this when he watched a video of moves that he had not learned. Watching videos of sports can be useful practice!

Sports psychologists help athletes prepare their minds to compete. This is just as important as preparing the body. Athletes learn to picture what they want to happen in their heads, such as scoring a goal or hitting a target. This technique can help them succeed.

When dancers see a move that they already know how to perform, their brains respond to it in the same way as if they were actually dancing.

Racers pass the baton in an Olympic relay. The winners are often the team that have practiced this difficult stage of the race a lot during training.

HARD TRAINING

Athletes must train in the same conditions as they will be competing. If they are racing at high **altitude**, the air will be thinner. This makes it harder for the body to get enough oxygen. Some athletes do all their early fitness training at high altitudes. It makes them even stronger at low altitudes.

START TO TRAIN

A training program is designed for a certain sport and a certain athlete. It changes every day, and the athlete will concentrate on different things as a competition approaches.

Track athletes work out about 20 hours a week. To start with, they do base training. That gets their bodies into a good condition. Base training lasts four to eight weeks. It includes 10 percent speed work and 15 percent strength exercise. The other 75 percent of training is designed to increase the athletes' **endurance**.

OVER THE EDGE

Athletes must be careful not to overtrain. Pushing your body too hard causes health problems. **Coordination** can suffer: you are too tired to concentrate, and you may keep making the same mistakes. Your body can also get weaker. Athletes who have overtrained need to rest and let their bodies heal.

A cross-training machine copies the movements of running and works the arms and legs at the same time.

Every fourth week, runners take a rest so their bodies can recover. They run fewer miles and reduce the hours in the gym.

HIT THE PEAK

As the event gets closer, the athletes want to be running faster and faster so they are at their peak for the big race. They train slightly less so they can recover quickly. World-class athletes run in small races as part of their buildup for the major competition.

SPORTS TECHNOLOGY

Technology helps athletes perform better. You may think sports are just about great players, but technology plays a very important part too.

Most sports would not be as exciting without the latest **technology**. For example, the first ice hockey skates were metal blades tied to the bottoms of shoes. This made stopping and turning difficult. The first sticks were thin pieces of wood, making fancy stick-play next to impossible. Even the ice is better because of technology. Once, the sport was only played on rough and uneven frozen lakes. This made play difficult—not to mention dangerous! Today, teams play year-round on smooth, indoor ice rinks.

MATERIALS

Athletes use equipment made of several special **fabrics**. Shoes are designed specially for each sport. There are high jump shoes, sprinting shoes, javelin shoes, and others. Cycling helmets used for safety are also **aerodynamic**. This reduces wind resistance, so cyclists can go faster. The helmet has vents to help keep riders cool.

HIGH-TECH

We use computers every day. So do athletes. Computers time their events and take video so the athletes can play them back. When athletes are hurt, computers help doctors look at the injuries and reduce recovery time.

Behind a high-speed game of ice hockey is a lot of high-tech equipment.

AIR FLOW

Wind tunnels are long tubes built to study aerodynamics. Instruments collect information when wind is blown over an object. The information is used to make improvements to sports equipment. Aerodynamics are important in many sports, from ski-jumping to motor racing.

FANTASTIC FABRIC

Athletes use many amazing materials to help them get an advantage. Downhill skiers wear skintight suits that reduce **drag** as they whizz down the mountain. The suits are made from fabrics that suck the sweat away from the body. That stops the skiers from getting too cold.

Fabrics also make athletes safer. Ice hockey goalies wear pads. These are full of soft foam. The outside is leather and nylon, so water from the ice does not get inside.

REAL LIFE

Many of the swimmers at the 2008 Olympics raced in a new type of swimsuit that covered the whole body and head. The suits **repel** water so the swimmer can power through the water faster. The suits also squeeze the main muscles used by the swimmer. This prevents injuries and helps the muscles recover after a tough race.

This racket is made from the latest flexible materials, but it also has a very simple improvement: the squarer shape makes it easier to hit balls in the corner of the racketball court.

WOOD OR NOT?

Once, most sports equipment was made of wood. However, wood is heavy and breaks easily. In the last 20 years, wood has been replaced by lighter and stronger materials, such as carbon fiber, aluminum, and titanium. These materials are now used in many things, from tennis rackets to hockey sticks.

However, some sports equipment is still wooden. The best cricket bats are made from willow wood, and top baseballers use bats made from maple and ash. Champion skateboarders use boards made from thin layers of maple glued together. No other material, not even the most high-tech plastics, have the combination of strength and flexibility that a wooden board has.

A speed skier tests his suit in a wind tunnel. The streamlined outfit allows a skier to travel downhill at 125 miles per hour (200 km/h). That is faster than a falling skydiver!

REAL LIFE

Technology helps athletes with disabilities. A leg **prosthesis** used to be shaped to look like a real leg. Now, disabled runners use special prostheses built for sprinting. They are carbon-fiber springs with no heel. This technology helps disabled sprinters reach Olympic speeds.

COMPUTER JUDGES

Many kinds of motor racing are so fast that it is sometimes difficult to see who is the winner, or if someone is cheating. An electric eye watches the start. If a driver jumps the green light, he or she gets a penalty or is **disqualified**. The eye has an invisible beam that runs across the track to a **detector**. When the car breaks the beam, the computer knows it has crossed the line.

REAL LIFE

Tennis courts are fitted with the Hawk-Eye system. Hawk-Eye uses computer-linked cameras to record the movements of balls around the court. The computer then creates a video of the game in **3-D**. Officials use Hawk-Eye for close line calls. For players and spectators, it provides another way of watching important replays from the match.

A computer image is the only way of seeing who will win this race. The "photo-finish" picture shows that the lower sprinter is going to cross the line first.

This way the timing of races is so precise it can measure in thousandths of a second.

Computers are good for collecting other information. Athletes can use watches that have heart rate monitors. While the athlete works out, information about heart rate, speed, distance, and energy used is recorded. It is sent to a computer and used to adjust training.

GOLF GAMES

Computers help golfers with practice too. **Simulators** allow golfers to train indoors. Players hit balls toward a screen (right) displaying a golf course, and a computers tells them where the ball would land.

GLOSSARY

3-D Short for "three dimensions," meaning you can see all the way around something

aerobic The way cells release energy using oxygen

aerodynamic Something that is designed so air flows around it easily

altitude How high somewhere is above sea level

anaerobic A form of energy production in cells that does not need oxygen

calcium A metal that is part of hard body structures, such as bones and teeth

carbohydrate A food type that includes sugars and starches

cells Small units that are grouped together to make a body. There are trillions of cells in a human body

conscious Something that is done after a person has thought about it

coordination Being able to move separate parts of the body at the same time

dehydrated When the body runs out of water

detector A machine that detects, or picks up, something

disqualified Removed from a race or competition for breaking the rules

drag The force of air pushing against an object, slowing it down

endurance Being able to carry on for a long time without getting too tired

fabric A material used to make clothing

fibers Thin threads

flexibility How much your body can move, bend, or twist

hormone A substance in the body that controls how it works. Hormones control growth

kinesiology Studying how the shape and structure of the body allows it to move

minerals Simple chemicals that are used by the body

motivated To have a reason for doing something

muscle fibers Threads of fibrous tissue that have the ability to contract

nerve Bundles of fibers that carry messages between the brain and spinal cord and other parts of the body

nutrients Useful substances in food or drink

oxygen A gas in the air that is used by the body to burn food and release the energy stored inside

prosthesis A replacement body part

proteins Substances used by the body to build muscles and also inside cells to run body processes

psychologists People who study the mind, the part of a person that thinks and has emotions

pulse The rhythm of the heart's beat that can be felt in certain blood vessels

repel To push away

saturated fat A solid fat, most often found in meat

simulator A computer program that recreates a real thing onscreen

steroid A type of drug that works like a hormone to make the body's muscles grow faster

supplement A substance that athletes eat or drink, which helps their bodies recover from training

technique The way you do something

technology When science is used to make something useful

tendons Tough strings or cords that join muscles to bones

unconscious Describes something that occurs automatically without a person thinking about it

unsaturated fat An oily fat made in plants and some animals, such as fish

vitamins Food chemicals that have many uses in the body

voluntary Describes something that people decide they want to do

FURTHER INFORMATION

Books

Boomerangs, Blades, and Basketballs by Jayne Creighton. Austin, TX: Raintree Steck-Vaughn, 2000.

Extreme Sports by John Crossingham. New York, NY: Crabtree Publishing, 2004.

The Leaping, Sliding, Sprinting, Riding Science Book: 50 Super Sports Science Activities by Bobby Mercer. New York, NY: Lark Books, 2006.

Sports by Ian Graham. Austin, TX: Raintree Steck-Vaughn, 1995.

Sports for Life: How Athletes Have More Fun by Robin Roberts. Brookfield, CN: Millbrook Press, 2000.

Sports Lab: How Science Has Changed Sports by Robert Sheely. New York, NY: Silver Moon, 1994.

Websites

Gatoraid Sports Science Institute:
http://www.gssiweb.com

Museum of Science, Art, and Human Perception:
http://www.exploratorium.edu/sports

National Geographic Sports Video:
http://video.nationalgeographic.com/video/player/places/culture-places/sports

Sports Science Project Ideas:
http://www.sciencebuddies.org/science-fairprojects/project_ideas/home_Sports.shtml

Whyfiles: Whack That Baseball!:
http://whyfiles.org/interactives/index.php?g=5.txt

Printed in the U.S.A.